Have You Seen an ELEPHANT?

To the bravest little explorer, Sofia Isabelle Parton – E.E.

Published in Canada and the U.S. by Kids Can Press Ltd.
25 Dockside Drive, Toronto, ON M5A 0B5

Kids Can Press is a Corus Entertainment Inc. company

www.kidscanpress.com

The artwork in this book was rendered digitally.
The text is set in Pleuf Pro.

Edited by Patricia Ocampo
Designed by Marie Bartholomew

Printed and bound in Buji, Shenzhen, China, in 10/2023 by WKT Company

CM 24 0 9 8 7 6 5 4 3 2 1

Library and Archives Canada Cataloguing in Publication

Title: Have you seen an elephant? / Elina Ellis.
Names: Ellis, Elina, author, illustrator.
Description: Series statement: Alex's field guides ; 1
Identifiers: Canadiana 20230440711 | ISBN 9781525306747 (hardcover)
Subjects: LCSH: Elephants–Juvenile literature. | LCSH: Endangered species–Juvenile literature.
Classification: LCC QL737.P98 E45 2024 | DDC j599.67168–dc23

Kids Can Press gratefully acknowledges that the land on which our office is located is the traditional territory of many nations, including the Mississaugas of the Credit, the Anishnabeg, the Chippewa, the Haudenosaunee and the Wendat peoples, and is now home to many diverse First Nations, Inuit and Métis peoples.

We thank the Government of Ontario, through Ontario Creates, the Ontario Arts Council; the Canada Council for the Arts; and the Government of Canada for supporting our publishing activity.

MIX
Paper | Supporting responsible forestry
FSC
www.fsc.org   FSC® C010256

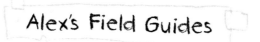

Alex's Field Guides

Have You Seen an ELEPHANT?

Elina Ellis

Kids Can Press

Hello, my name is Alex.

I am an explorer, and
I LOVE ELEPHANTS!

I know everything about them. So I've decided
to set out on an expedition to find some real elephants
and say HELLO. How hard could it be?

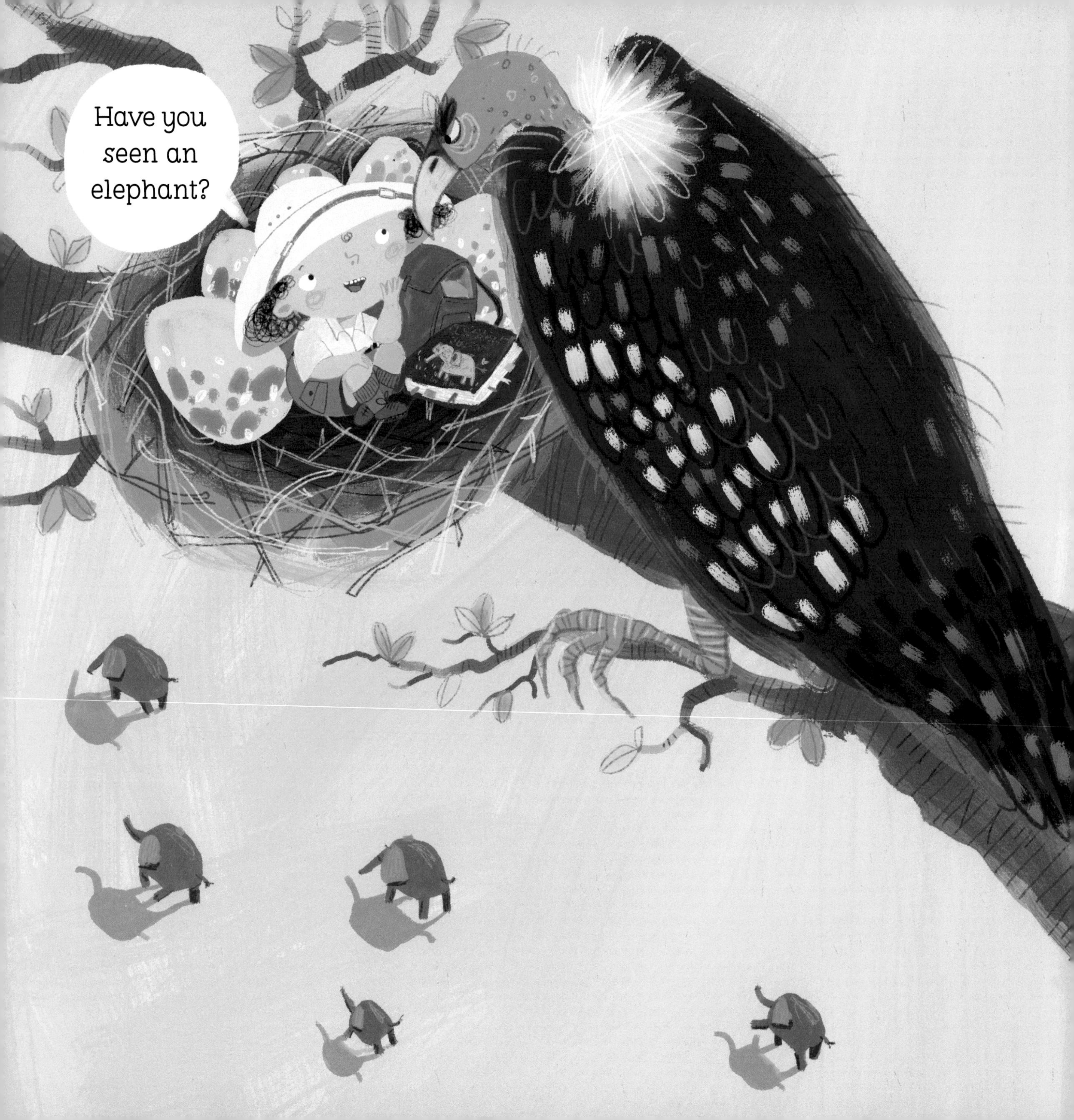
Have you seen an elephant?

Did you know that elephants
have poor digestive systems?

That's why they are always full of gas!

Have a look in my journal.

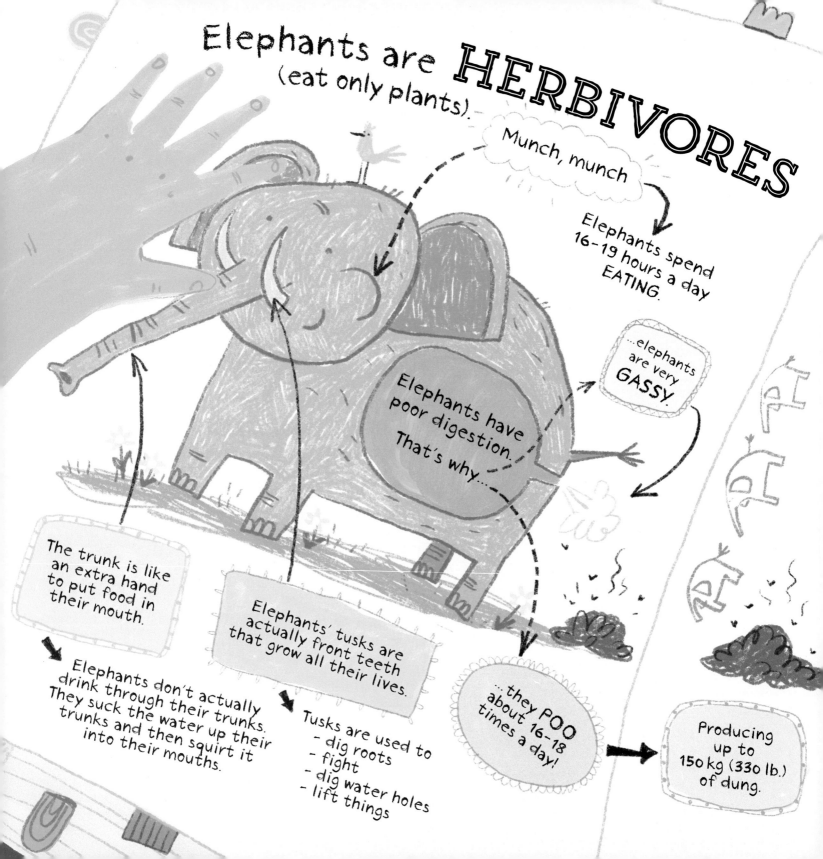

Elephants are HERBIVORES
(eat only plants).

Munch, munch

Elephants spend 16-19 hours a day EATING.

Elephants have poor digestion. That's why...

...elephants are very GASSY.

The trunk is like an extra hand to put food in their mouth.

Elephants don't actually drink through their trunks. They suck the water up their trunks and then squirt it into their mouths.

Elephants' tusks are actually front teeth that grow all their lives.

Tusks are used to
- dig roots
- fight
- dig water holes
- lift things

...they POO about 16-18 times a day!

Producing up to 150 kg (330 lb.) of dung.

Where are all the elephants?

Elephants are VERY INTELLIGENT.

Mama ♥ Cousin Friendly human Tasty bush

Elephants have a good memory. They remember friends and places for years.

Elephants have great hearing.

They can hear other elephants up to 10 km (6 mi.) away.

The nerves in their feet pick up vibrations from the ground.

That's ME!

They can recognize their own reflection.

Elephants are as SMART as Dolphins AND Apes

They also have the BIGGEST BRAIN on land.

Elephant brain 5 kg (11 lb.)

Dolphin brain 1.6 kg (3.5 lb.)

Human brain 1.4 kg (3 lb.)

Gorilla brain 0.5 kg (1.1 lb.)

There are still
no elephants
in sight ...

Elephants are so hard to find.
Maybe I should start looking for

TIGERS.

I LOVE TIGERS!
I know everything about them.

Have you
seen a
TIGER?

HOW TO MAKE YOUR OWN JOURNAL

CHOOSE YOUR
FAVORITE ANIMAL:

PREPARE SUPPLIES:
- ☒ journal
- ☒ colored pens and pencils
- ☒ ruler, eraser and a pair of scissors
- ☒ glue, tape, stickers, sticky notes

START YOUR RESEARCH:

Watch TV programs
and documentaries.

Visit the zoo
or explore in nature.

Ask questions.

Read books and
magazines.

Note everything you find interesting and exciting in your journal.

YOU CAN:

Draw

Write

Collage

Create maps

Make diagrams

Use stickers and sticky notes

When you finish one journal, START ANOTHER ONE!

RESOURCES

HOW YOU CAN HELP

Alex might find it hard to find an elephant because there are fewer and fewer of them. The elephant is an endangered species, which means both the African and Asian elephant population is at risk of extinction. But you can help by donating, volunteering or getting involved in other ways.
Here are a few organizations who can assist:

- The David Sheldrick Wildlife Trust (www.sheldrickwildlifetrust.org)

- Game Rangers International (www.gamerangersinternational.org)

- Roots and Shoots (www.rootsandshoots.org)

- World Wildlife Fund (www.worldwildlife.org)

SELECTED SOURCES

◦ Britannica Online: www.britannica.com/animal/elephant-mammal

◦ EleAid (Supporting Asian Elephant Conservation): www.eleaid.com

◦ Elephants for Africa: www.elephantsforafrica.org

◦ Elephant Listening Project: www.elephantlisteningproject.org

◦ Elephant Voices: www.elephantvoices.org

◦ International Elephant Foundation: www.elephantconservation.org

◦ International Environment Library Consortium – African Elephants Fact Sheet: https://ielc.libguides.com/sdzg/factsheets/african_elephant/characteristics

◦ Real Clear Science: www.realclearscience.com/blog/2023/10/the-most-amazing-appendage-in-the-world.html

◦ Safaris Africana: www.safarisafricana.com/african-vs-asian-elephant/